If God Is Good...

Faith *in the* Midst *of* Suffering *and* Evil

RANDY ALCORN

MULTNOMAH
BOOKS

One hundred percent of the royalties from this book will be given to promote good, oppose evil, and relieve suffering around the world.

Other books by Randy Alcorn

CONTENTS

"What is the meaning of it, Watson?" said Holmes solemnly as he laid down the paper. "What object is served by this circle of misery and violence and fear? It must tend to some end, or else our universe is ruled by chance, which is unthinkable. But what end? There is the great standing perennial problem to which human reason is as far from an answer as ever."

—Sir Arthur Conan Doyle, *The Adventure of the Cardboard Box*

INTRODUCTION

A Note to Readers, Especially to Those Hurting and Confused

I got to know my friend Jim Harrell after he read my book *Heaven*. We talked on the phone, exchanged e-mails, and quickly connected at a heart level. Jim, a successful businessman, strong and athletic for most of his life, told me he really looked forward to reading this book. He asked me for the first draft, which I happily sent him.

Jim contracted ALS, Lou Gehrig's disease, in 2003. Yet Jim has called the last six years of his life the most significant. While his body deteriorated and he lost normal functions, one after another, Jim touched more people (and was touched more by God) than at any other time of his life.

While writing this book I drew on Jim's wisdom, as well as that of many other sufferers.

During the two years it has taken me to research and write this book, many people have asked about the project. I expected that my answer, containing the words *evil* and *suffering,* would prompt a quick change of subject. Most, however, expressed keen interest and asked penetrating questions. Several launched into their own stories, as if having received permission to uncork the bottle.

What, after all, is more universal to human experience than suffering? And what is more important than the perspective we bring to it?

How we answer this book's central question will radically affect how we see God and the world around us.

We may want to turn away from world suffering and refuse to reflect on the significance of our own pain; we just want it to go away. But despite the superficiality of our culture, we remain God's image-bearers—thinking and caring people, wired to ask questions and seek answers.

No question looms larger than the central question of this book: If God is good...*why all this evil and suffering*? If God loves us, how can he justify allowing (or sending) the sometimes overwhelming difficulties we face?

Does this great question interest you? If so, I invite you to join me on a journey of discovery.

While traveling this long road, I found something surprising: the journey was not only rewarding, but fascinating, enlightening, and at times downright enjoyable. I know it sounds counterintuitive—shouldn't it *depress* someone to meditate on evil and suffering? In fact, I'd already seen enough evil and suffering to feel deeply troubled. What I needed was *perspective*. Instead of being disheartened, I'm encouraged.

In this process, I've taken the most pleasure in focusing on God, exploring his attributes of goodness, love, holiness, justice, patience, grace, and mercy. While my journey hasn't unearthed easy answers, I'm astonished at how much insight Scripture offers.

Seeking answers to this question should turn us toward Jesus in a fresh way.

In looking for answers, I've beheld a God who says, "I have indeed seen the misery of my people in Egypt. I have heard them crying out because of their slave drivers, and I am concerned about their suffering" (Exodus 3:7). I've found great comfort in hearing God speak of a time when he could bear his people's misery no longer (see Judges 10:16). I revel in God's emphatic promise that he will make a New Earth where he will come down to live with us, and on which "he will wipe every tear from their eyes. There will be no more death or mourning or crying or pain" (Revelation 21:4). Above all, in this process, I've seen Jesus.

The first physician to die of the AIDS virus in the United Kingdom was a young Christian. He contracted the disease while conducting medical research in Zimbabwe. In the last days of his life he struggled to express himself to his wife. Near the end, he couldn't talk, and had only enough strength to write the letter *J*.

She ran through her mental dictionary, saying various words beginning with J. None was right. Finally she said, "Jesus?"

He nodded. Yes, Jesus.

Jesus filled his thoughts. That's all he wanted to say. That's all his wife needed to hear.

In my research and writing, my thoughts too kept coming back to Jesus. What better place?

Often God has wiped away my own tears as I've contemplated potentially faith-jarring matters. I've been left, not in despair, but with great hope that defies description and a peace that transcends understanding (see Philippians 4:7).

This journey has stretched my trust in God and his purposes, and I have emerged better prepared to face suffering and help others because of it. I feel I have much more to offer believers who may be questioning their faith, as well as unbelievers who consider the problem of evil and suffering their single greatest obstacle to faith.

If you stay with this book until the end, I feel certain you'll be better for it. I believe God will reward you, as he has me, not only with much-needed perspective, but with deep-rooted peace and joy, and renewed perseverance.

We each bring our own burdens on the journey.

If abuse, rape, desertion, paralysis, debilitating disease, or the loss of a loved one has devastated you, then this issue isn't theoretical, philosophical, or theological. It's deeply personal. Logical arguments won't satisfy you; in fact, they might offend you. You need help with the *emotional* problem of evil, not merely the *logical* problem of evil.

Though I write personally, from the heart, and tell stories of great courage and perspective, I must also present a case from Scripture and appeal to logic. But remember this: you are a whole person, and the path to your heart travels through your mind. Truth matters. To touch us at the heart level—and to keep touching us over days, months, years, and decades—truth must work its way into our *minds.*

By all means, speak with a friend and perhaps a pastor or counselor. But in the process don't seek comfort by ignoring truth. When you try to soothe your feelings without bothering to think deeply about ideas, you are asking to be manipulated. Quick-fix feelings won't sustain you over the long haul. On the other hand, deeply rooted beliefs—specifically a worldview grounded in Scripture—will allow you to persevere and hold on to a faith built on the rock of God's truth.

In writing his magnificent story of redemption, God has revealed truths about himself, us, the world, heaven and hell, goodness, evil, and suffering. Those truths teem with life. The blood of man and God flows through them. God speaks with passion, not indifference; he utters fascinating words, not dull ones. To come to grips with the problem of evil and suffering, you must do more than hear heart-wrenching stories about suffering people. You must hear God's truth to help you interpret those stories.

Maybe you're holding on to years of bitterness and depression. You blame someone for your suffering—and that someone may be God. You will not find relief unless you gain perspective.

Or perhaps you fear that any attempt to "gain perspective" will deny or minimize your suffering, or that of others. I promise you, the Bible doesn't minimize suffering or gloss over it, and neither will I.

At times, each of us must snuggle into our Father's arms, like children, and there receive the comfort we need. Joni Eareckson Tada and Steve Estes write,

God, like a father, doesn't just give advice. He gives himself. He becomes the husband to the grieving widow (Isaiah 54:5). He becomes the comforter to the barren woman (Isaiah 54:1). He becomes the father of the orphaned (Psalm 10:14). He becomes the bridegroom to the single person (Isaiah 62:5). He is the healer to the sick (Exodus 15:26). He is the wonderful counselor to the confused and depressed (Isaiah 9:6).[1]

The faith that can't be shaken is the faith that has been shaken.

God tells us that trials in which evil and suffering come upon us "have come so that your faith—of greater worth than gold, which perishes even though refined by fire—may be proved genuine and may result in praise, glory and honor when Jesus Christ is revealed" (1 Peter 1:7).

Alice Gray writes of sitting at a restaurant, talking with a friend about painful challenges in their lives. They frequently mentioned the Lord.

Alice noticed a young woman at the next table with a radiant, joyful face. The young woman smiled and said she'd overheard their conversation. Speaking softly, she encouraged Alice and Marlene that God understood and cared about their heartaches, and nothing could separate them from God's love.

Alice continued talking with Marlene but realized something was different. The young woman's words had refreshed them. When the smiling woman got up to leave, Alice noticed she wore bulky shoes, carried a walking stick, and moved with a severe limp.

The waitress told Alice this woman had been in a near-fatal automobile accident the year before. She'd been in and out of the hospital and rehabilitation. Her husband divorced her, their home had been sold, and she'd just moved into her own apartment. She used public transportation because she couldn't drive. She'd been unable to find a job.

Alice sat stunned. She says, "This young woman's conversation had been filled with delights of the Lord. There had been no weariness about her. She had encouraged us with words of praise and promise. Meeting her that day, we never would have suspected that storms were raging in her life. Even as she stepped outside into the cold winter wind, she seemed to carry God's warm shelter of hope with her."

God's Word is central to gaining an eternal perspective.

In times of crisis we try to make sense of life. We crave perspective for our minds and relief for our hearts. We need our worldview realigned by God's inspired Word: "All Scripture is God-breathed and is useful for teaching, rebuking, correcting and training in righteousness" (2 Timothy 3:16).

I quote Scripture frequently in this book because God promises that his Word "will not return to me empty, but will accomplish what I desire and achieve the purpose for which I sent it" (Isaiah 55:11). God never makes such a promise about my words or your words. I want this book to accomplish God's purpose—and that will happen only if it remains faithful to his words.

This book won't work magic or make your problems disappear. But I hope

God will use it to help you, regardless of the difficulties you face. He offers us profound, moving, and surprising insights that can feed our minds, warm our hearts, and give us the strength to face a world that is not what it once was, or what it one day will be. I pray that readers of *If God Is Good* will not only find help for themselves, but life-changing insights to share with others—believers and unbelievers, family and friends and neighbors and co-workers—in their time of greatest need.

SECTION 1

Understanding the Problem of Evil and Suffering

I

WHY IS THE PROBLEM OF EVIL AND SUFFERING SO IMPORTANT?

The problem of evil and suffering moves from the philosophical to the personal in a moment of time.

In my research I read all sorts of books—philosophical, theological, practical, and personal. It's one thing to talk about evil and suffering philosophically; it's another to live with it. Philosophy professor Peter Van Inwagen writes,

> Angels may weep because the world is filled with suffering. A human being weeps because his daughter, she and not another, has died of leukemia this very night, or because her village, the only world she knows, is burning and the mutilated bodies of her husband and her son lie at her feet.[1]

Three weeks after his thirty-three-year-old son died in a car crash, pastor and evangelist Greg Laurie addressed a crowd of twenty-nine thousand at Angel Stadium in Anaheim, California. "I've talked about heaven my whole life," Laurie said, "and I've given many messages on life after death. I've counseled many people who have lost a loved one and I thought I knew a little bit about it. But I have to say that when it happens to you, it's a whole new world." The day his son died, he told the crowd, was "the hardest day of my life."[2]

Pain is always local. It has a face and a name.

The American response to September 11, 2001, demonstrated that large-scale evil and suffering usually remain distant from us.

In Sudan, millions, including children, have been murdered, raped, and enslaved.

The 2004 Asian tsunami killed more than 280,000 people. Malaria causes more than two million fatalities annually, the majority of them African children. Around the world, some 26,500 children die every day; that's eighteen every minute.

The loss of American lives in the terrorist attacks of September 11, 2001, numbered 2,973—horrible indeed, yet a small fraction of the terror and loss of life faced around the world. The death toll in the 1994 Rwandan genocide, for example, amounted to more than *two* World Trade Center disasters *every day for one hundred days straight.* Americans discovered in one day, and some seemed to forget quickly, what much of the world already knew—violent death comes quickly, hits hard, and can be unspeakably awful.

If we open our eyes, we'll see the problem of evil and suffering even when it doesn't touch us directly.

A friend of ours spoke at a Christian gathering. Afterward, on her way to her car, someone raped her. She became pregnant and gave birth to her first child. Because racial differences would have made it clear her husband hadn't fathered the baby, the couple put the infant up for adoption. Since then they've been unable to have another child. Her lifelong dream of raising children remains unfulfilled.

I once had to tell a wife, son, and daughter that their husband and father had died on a hunting trip. I still remember the anguished face of the little girl, then hearing her wail, "Not Daddy, no, not Daddy!"

Years ago I had to tell my mother that her only brother had been murdered with a meat cleaver.

A Christian woman tipped over on her riding lawn mower and fell into a pond. The machine landed on top of her, pinning her to the bottom and drowning her. Such a bizarre death prompted some to ask, "Why, God?" and "Why like this?"

After his wife died, in great pain C. S. Lewis realized, "If I had really cared, as I thought I did, about the sorrows of the world, I should not have been so overwhelmed when my own sorrow came."[3]

Our own suffering is often our wake-up call. But even if you aren't now facing it, look around and you'll see many who are.

WHY TALK ABOUT THE PROBLEM?

More people point to the problem of evil and suffering as their reason for not believing in God than any other—it is not merely a problem, it is *the* problem.

A Barna poll asked, "If you could ask God only one question and you knew he would give you an answer, what would you ask?" The most common response was, "Why is there pain and suffering in the world?"[4]

John Stott says,

> The fact of suffering undoubtedly constitutes the single greatest challenge
> to the Christian faith, and has been in every generation. Its distribution and
> degree appear to be entirely random and therefore unfair. Sensitive spirits
> ask if it can possibly be reconciled with God's justice and love.[5]

Richard Swinburne, writing in the *Oxford Companion to Philosophy*, says the problem of evil is *"the most powerful objection to traditional theism."*[6]

Ronald Nash writes, "Objections to theism come and go.... But every philosopher I know believes that the most serious challenge to theism was, is, and will continue to be the problem of evil."[7]

You will not get far in a conversation with someone who rejects the Christian faith before the problem of evil is raised. Pulled out like the ultimate trump card, it's supposed to silence believers and prove that the all-good and all-powerful God of the Bible doesn't exist.

The problem of evil is atheism's cornerstone.

German playwright Georg Büchner (1813–37) called the problem of evil, "the rock of atheism." Atheists point to the problem of evil as proof that the God of the Bible doesn't exist. Every day the ancient argument gets raised in college philosophy classes, coffee shops, dinner discussions, e-mail exchanges, blogs, talk shows, and best-selling books.

Atheists write page after page about evil and suffering. The problem of evil never strays far from their view; it intrudes upon chapters with vastly different subjects. It's one of the central reasons Sam Harris writes, "Atheism is not a philosophy; it is not even a view of the world; it is simply an admission of the obvious."[8] Harris then scolds Christians, saying about intelligent people (such as himself), "We stand dumbstruck by *you*—by your denial of tangible reality, by the suffering you create in service to your religious myths, and by your attachment to an imaginary God."[9] (At least we know what he's thinking!)

Many suppose that scientific evidence is the cornerstone of atheism. But the famous one-time champion of atheism, Britain's Anthony Flew, renounced his atheism due to the complexity of the universe and his belief in the overwhelming evidence for intelligent design. After examining Richard Dawkins's reasoning in *The God Delusion*—that the origin of life can be attributed to a "lucky chance"— Flew said, "If that's the best argument you have, then the game is over." However, although he abandoned his atheism, Flew did not convert to the Christian faith, but to deism. Why? Flew could not get past the problem of evil. He believes that there has to be a God who created the universe, but then must have abandoned it.

A faith that leaves us unprepared for suffering is a false faith that deserves to be lost.

A lot of bad theology inevitably surfaces when we face suffering. John Piper writes, "Wimpy worldviews make wimpy Christians. And wimpy Christians won't survive the days ahead."[10]

Auschwitz survivor Viktor Frankl wrote, "Just as the small fire is extinguished by the storm whereas a large fire is enhanced by it, likewise a weak faith is weakened by predicaments and catastrophes whereas a strong faith is strengthened by them."[11] When people lose their faith because of suffering, it's usually a weak or nominal faith that doesn't account for or prepare them for evil and suffering. I believe that any faith not based on the truth needs to be lost. The sooner, the better.

Believing God exists is not the same as trusting the God who exists. A nominal Christian often discovers in suffering that his faith has been misplaced. It's been in his church, denomination, or family tradition, but not Christ. As he faces evil and suffering, he may lose his faith. But that's actually a good thing. I have sympathy for people who lose their faith, but any faith lost in suffering wasn't a faith worth keeping. (Genuine faith will be tested; false faith will be lost.)

If you base your faith on lack of affliction, your faith lives on the brink of extinction and will fall apart because of a frightening diagnosis or a shattering phone call. Token faiths will not survive suffering, nor should they. Only when they get cleared away can true faith replace them.

Suffering and evil exert a force that either pushes us away from God or pulls us toward him. I know a man who lost his faith after facing terrible evil, suffering, and injustice. My heart breaks for him, and I pray that my family and I will never suffer what he did. But if personal suffering gives sufficient evidence that God doesn't exist, then surely I shouldn't wait until *I* suffer to conclude he's a myth. If *my* suffering would one day justify denying God, then I should deny him now in light of *other* people's suffering.

The devastation of tragedy feels just as real for people whose faith endures suffering. But because they know that others have suffered and learned to trust God anyway, they can apply that trust to God as they face their own disasters. Because they do not place their hope for health and abundance and secure relationships in this life, but in an eternal life to come, their hope remains firm regardless of what happens.

Losing your faith may be God's gift to you. Only when you jettison ungrounded and untrue faith can you replace it with valid faith in the true God— faith that can pass, and even find strength in, the most formidable of life's tests.

In her moving book *The Year of Magical Thinking,* Joan Didion writes about the sudden, unexpected death of her husband. As I read, my heart broke not only for what happened to her, but for the first six words of the book's concluding sentence: "No eye is on the sparrow."[12]

Didion apparently means that so far as she can tell, there is no God, or at least, no God who cares and watches over us. I think she's just a normal hurting person who needs men and women around her who can see God in the midst of their suffering, so they might help her see him in hers.

Suffering will come; we owe it to God, ourselves, and those around us to prepare for it.

Live long enough and you *will* suffer. In this life, the only way to avoid suffering is to die.

Bethany Hamilton grew up surfing on the island of Kauai, Hawaii. At age five she chose to follow Jesus. When she was thirteen, a fourteen-foot tiger shark attacked her, severing one of her arms. Bethany returned to surfing one month later. A year later, despite her disability, she won her first national title.

Bethany says, "It was Jesus Christ who gave me peace when I got attacked by the shark.... And it was what God had taught me growing up that helped me overcome my fears...to get back into the water to keep surfing."

She continues, "My mom and I were praying before the shark attack that God would use me. Well, to me, 1 Timothy 1:12 kind of tells me that God considered me faithful enough to appoint me to his service. I just want to say that no matter who you are, God can use you even if you think you're not the kind of person that can be used. You might think: why would God use me? That's what I thought.... I was like thirteen and there God goes using me!"

Bethany and her parents had given careful thought to the God they served and his sovereign purposes. Obviously not every tragedy leads to winning a national title, but Bethany began where all of us can, by trusting God; in her case, with a support system of people having an eternal perspective. Hence, she was prepared to face suffering when it came, and to emerge stronger.

Unfortunately, most evangelical churches—whether traditional, liturgical, or emergent—have failed to teach people to think biblically about the realities of evil and suffering. A pastor's daughter told me, "I was never taught the Christian life was going to be difficult. I've discovered it is, and I wasn't ready."

A young woman battling cancer wrote me, "I was surprised that when it happened, it was hard and it hurt and I was sad and I couldn't find anything good or redeeming about my losses. I never expected that a Christian who had access to God could feel so empty and alone."

Our failure to teach a biblical theology of suffering leaves Christians unprepared for harsh realities. It also leaves our children vulnerable to history, philosophy, and global studies classes that raise the problems of evil and suffering while denying the Christian worldview. Since the question *will* be raised, shouldn't Christian parents and churches raise it first and take people to Scripture to see what God says about it?

Most of us don't give focused thought to evil and suffering until we experience them. This forces us to formulate perspective on the fly, at a time when our thinking is muddled and we're exhausted and consumed by pressing issues. Readers who have "been there" will attest that it's far better to think through suffering in advance.

Sometimes sufferers reach out for answers to those woefully unprepared. A physician's assistant friend of ours wrote,

> When I was admitted to the hospital in sepsis with a 50/50 chance of survival, I asked the chaplain how we could believe that God is love, when this felt like the antithesis of love. I said I wouldn't inflict this much suffering on someone I hated, let alone someone I loved. She told me she would "look it up," then left my room and never came back. I posed the same question to the social worker who came to visit me a few days later. She told me that God's like a giant and we're like little ants, and sometimes He accidentally steps on our ant hills and some of us get hurt. She said our suffering is random and God's probably not even aware of it.

Pastor James Montgomery Boice had a clearer perspective. Diagnosed with liver cancer, he stood before his Philadelphia church in May 2000. After explaining his illness he said,

> Should you pray for a miracle? Well, you're free to do that, of course. My general impression is that the God who is able to do miracles—and He certainly can—is also able to keep you from getting the problem in the first place. So although miracles do happen, they're rare by definition.... Above all, I would say pray for the glory of God. If you think of God glorifying Himself in history and you say, where in all of history has God most glorified Himself? He did it at the cross of Jesus Christ, and it wasn't by delivering Jesus from the cross, though He could have....

God is in charge. When things like this come into our lives, they are not accidental. It's not as if God somehow forgot what was going on, and something bad slipped by.... God is not only the one who is in charge; God is also good. Everything He does is good.... If God does something in your life, would you change it? If you'd change it, you'd make it worse. It wouldn't be as good.[13]

Eight weeks later, having taught his people first how to live and then how to die, Pastor Boice departed this world to "be with Christ, which is better by far" (Philippians 1:23).

On the other side of death, God promises that all who know him will experience acceptance into the arms of a holy, loving, and gracious God—the greatest miracle, the answer to the problem of evil and suffering. He promises us an eternal kingdom on the New Earth, where he says of those who come to trust him in this present world of evil and suffering, "They will be his people, and God himself will be with them and be their God. He will wipe every tear from their eyes. There will be no more death or mourning or crying or pain" (Revelation 21:3–4).